Briefly: John Stuart Mill's *Utilitarianism*

CITY OF LONDON SCHOOL

Name	Form	Date

Briefly: John Stuart Mill's *Utilitarianism*

David Mills Daniel

scm press

All rights reserved. No part of this publication may be
reproduced, stored in a retrieval system, or transmitted,
in any form or by any means, electronic, mechanical,
photocopying or otherwise, without the prior
permission of the publisher, SCM Press.

© David Mills Daniel 2006

The author and publisher acknowledge material
reproduced from G. Sher, ed., *Mill: Utilitarianism*,
2nd edition, Hackett, 2001. Reprinted by permission of
Hackett Publishing Company, Inc. All rights reserved.

British Library Cataloguing in Publication data

A catalogue record for this book is available
from the British Library

0 334 04027 2/9780 334 04027 9

First published in 2006 by SCM Press
9–17 St Alban's Place,
London N1 0NX

www.scm-canterburypress.co.uk

SCM Press is a division of
SCM-Canterbury Press Ltd

Printed and bound in Great Britain by
CPD (Wales) Ltd, Ebbw Vale

To My Wife

Contents

Introduction

The SCM *Briefly* series is designed to enable students and general readers to acquire knowledge and understanding of key texts in philosophy, philosophy of religion, theology and ethics. While the series will be especially helpful to those following university and A-level courses in philosophy, ethics and religious studies, it will in fact be of interest to anyone looking for a short guide to the ideas of a particular philosopher or theologian.

Each book in the series takes a piece of work by one philosopher and provides a summary of the original text, which adheres closely to it, and contains direct quotations from it, thus enabling the reader to follow each development in the philosopher's argument(s). Throughout the summary, there are page references to the original philosophical writing, so that the reader has ready access to the primary text. In the Introduction to each book, you will find details of the edition of the philosophical work referred to.

In *Briefly: Mill's Utilitarianism*, we refer to John Stuart Mill, *Utilitarianism*, edited by George Sher, second edition, Indianapolis/Cambridge: Hackett Publishing, 2001, ISBN 087220605x.

Each *Briefly* begins with an Introduction, followed by a chapter on the Context in which the work was written. Who was this writer? Why was this book written? With some Issues

Introduction

to Consider, and some Suggested Further Reading, this *Briefly* aims to get anyone started in their philosophical investigation. The detailed summary of the philosophical work is followed by a concise chapter-by-chapter overview and an extensive glossary of terms.

All words that appear in the Glossary are highlighted in bold type the first time that they appear in the Detailed Summary and the Overview of this *Briefly* guide.

Context

Who was John Stuart Mill?

John Stuart Mill was born in London in 1806, and was the son of James Mill, the utilitarian philosopher and friend of Jeremy Bentham, the founder of utilitarianism. The education that Mill received from his father, and which he describes in his *Autobiography*, was unusually ambitious. He started Greek and Latin when he was a few years old, lacked friends of his own age, and did not take part in sport; and this intense programme may have contributed to the severe depression he suffered when he was about 20. In 1823, Mill joined the East India Company, which at that time governed India, where he worked until the British government took over responsibility for India in 1858. During this time, Mill was developing, and writing about, his views on philosophical and political issues, and working out his own version of utilitarianism. *On Liberty* (1859), *Utilitarianism* (1861), *Considerations on Representative Government* (1861) and *The Subjection of Women* (1869) have had a major and continuing influence on moral and political philosophy, as well as on thinking about the rights of individuals and minorities, and the relationship between the individual and the state. Mill married Mrs Harriet Taylor, whom he had known for more than 20 years, in 1851, and was Liberal MP for Westminster between 1865 and 1868. He died in France in 1873.

What is *Utilitarianism?*

In *Utilitarianism,* Mill makes out a case for a consequentialist theory of ethics: that actions are not right or wrong in themselves, but are judged to be right or wrong according to their consequences. For Mill, the fundamental principle of morality is the utilitarian one: that actions are right to the extent that they promote pleasure and happiness, and wrong to the extent that they cause pain. However, Mill's version of utilitarianism differs from that of Bentham and his father. His concern was not solely with quantity of pleasure and determining the rightness or wrongness of actions through attempts to calculate the amounts of pleasure or pain that different possible courses of action might produce. He believed that there are grades or levels of pleasure, and that those associated with the mind, such as literary and artistic pursuits, are more valuable than purely physical ones, such as eating and drinking.

That intellectual pleasures are more valuable than physical ones is shown, he believed, by the fact that those who have experienced both think that they are, while such people are also qualified to decide which of any two pleasures is the more worthwhile. Those who enjoy intellectual pleasures may be more aware of life's imperfections, but they would not change places with those who do not. They would prefer, as Mill puts it, to be Socrates dissatisfied than a fool satisfied. Thus, Mill's version of utilitarianism is not open to the accusation of being hedonistic. Intellectual pleasures are rated above non-intellectual ones, while he emphasizes its unselfishness: utilitarians should be as concerned about the pleasures and happiness of others (general happiness), as they are about their own. Mill mentions the ideal of Jesus' golden rule: whatever you wish that people would do for you, do the same for them.

Mill deals with various objections to utilitarianism. He does not believe that happiness is unattainable, because it is not a permanent state of exalted pleasure that is being aimed at. He explains what he means by happiness: a well-balanced life, offering a range of (worthwhile) pleasures, little pain, enjoyment of family relationships and friendships and involvement in the wider affairs of society. And, with the social reforms and general improvement in the standard of living that were taking place in the nineteenth century, such a way of life was being achieved by growing numbers. He did not feel that it was unreasonable to ask people to be concerned about the happiness of others, because they are not expected to devote all their time to doing so. To the criticism that utilitarianism is godless, Mill's response is that it is consistent with God's purpose, if that purpose is (as Mill considers it should be) to ensure his creatures' happiness. He also points out that his version of utilitarianism does not require people to try to calculate the effects of all possible courses of action on the general happiness before they do anything. Established moral principles, such as those forbidding murder or theft, can be used, because experience has shown that, in general, they promote happiness. The fundamental principle of utility need only be invoked in situations where secondary principles conflict with each other.

But is this altogether satisfactory? At one level, Mill's argument for a hierarchy of pleasures is convincing. It seems only sensible to recognize qualitative as well as quantitative distinctions among pleasures. And it also seems to be the case that those who have experienced both intellectual and non-intellectual pleasures value the former more highly than the latter, and wish them to be accessible to, and enjoyed by, other people (which does not mean, as Mill seems to imply, that they will despise all non-intellectual ones). However, is a focus on pleasure and grades of pleasure, or even happiness, always relevant to moral decisions? Does it not accord more with our actual experience to relate much of morality and moral decision-making to meeting (the wide range of) human needs? And sometimes satisfying basic, non-intellectual needs takes priority over meeting intellectual ones, as when there are starving people who need to be fed. Mill also fails to explain why people ought to be as concerned for others' happiness as their own. He refers to concern for the happiness of others harmonizing with the obligations people naturally feel towards other members of society. But does not this invoke the moral principle of recognizing (and therefore treating) our fellow human beings as intrinsically valuable, as ends in themselves, not as a means to our own happiness?

Mill's handling of the relationship between utilitarianism and God's purpose is superficial, because it fails to recognize that, according to Christian teaching (Christianity is the religion Mill has in mind), God's purpose in creating the world was not just to make his creatures happy. There are problems, too, with using secondary moral principles. It may be sensible to do so, but it does mean that actions will be performed which will not create most happiness in that particular situation.

Mill wishes to prove the utilitarian view that happiness is both desirable and the only thing desirable as an end, and, therefore, that the principle of utility is the sole criterion of morality. The proof he offers is an analogy with visibility. Their being seen is the only proof that things are visible, so the only proof that something is desirable is that people desire it. People desire happiness individually, while general happiness is the happiness of the aggregate of all persons. Therefore, happiness is an end of human conduct, and the principle of utility (that actions are right to the extent that they promote pleasure and happiness, and wrong to the extent that they promote the reverse) a criterion of morality.

This so-called proof was criticized by G. E. Moore, in *Principia Ethica*, as involving a naturalistic fallacy: '"desirable" does not mean "able to be desired" as "visible" means "able to be seen" . . . [but] "what it is good to desire"; but when this is understood, it is no longer plausible to say that our only test of that, is what is actually desired'. But Mill does not seem to be attempting a strict proof that happiness is desirable as an end (indeed, he acknowledges that it would be impossible to do so), but rather inviting his readers to observe what their fellow human beings actually value. Happiness is obviously one of these things.

But is happiness the only thing people desire as an end, and, therefore, the sole criterion of morality? Mill argues that there is no real conflict with, for example, virtue, which people seem to desire as an end. Although happiness is the ultimate end, some things, like virtue, are good as a means to that end: virtuous utilitarians will seek to promote happiness. So, although utilitarians originally valued virtue because it helped to promote happiness, loving virtue (and thus promoting happiness) has now become so closely associated with happiness that it has become part of the end: part of what makes some people happy. Mill concludes that if human beings desire only things that are a part of, or a means to, happiness, it is the sole end of human action, while promoting happiness is the sole standard of morality; and he asks people to observe themselves and others, to see whether or not he is right.

However, although this is the way that utilitarians see virtue, it does not alter the fact that others connect virtue with doing things that are right in themselves, irrespective of whether or not they promote happiness. Further, there are those who will simply deny that happiness is the only, or even the most important thing, that they desire as an end: unless 'happiness' is just being used to embrace every possible end of human action.

Mill considers whether justice is, as some had claimed, a major obstacle to accepting utility as the criterion of right and wrong, and argues that justice does not appear to be an absolute standard, as people's ideas of it vary, and change over time. He analyses justice as consisting of: a rule or rules of conduct, which must be common to all human beings, and intended for their good; a desire to punish those who break the rule(s); and somebody whose rights under the rule(s) have been violated, and who can validly require society to uphold those rights. Mill acknowledges that justice is the most important part of morality, because it concerns moral rules, such as those forbidding people to hurt one another, which are central to human well-being, and which it is essential for society to enforce. But he maintains that utility is the reason why people should protect others' rights; only thus will all members of society have that security without which nothing can be enjoyed.

However, this does not seem to be an adequate account of justice. While it is true that ideas of what is just vary and change, at the root of the idea of justice, and attempting to be just, there seems to be recognition that human beings are entitled to fair and equal treatment, because they matter and are worthwhile in themselves.

There can be no doubt that happiness is one of the things that people desire, and it is difficult to ignore the effect on another person's, or other people's, happiness when deciding on a course of action. However, it is hard to accept that it is the only thing that people desire as an end, and that the principle of utility should be the sole criterion of morality. In *Utilitarianism*, Mill explicitly rejects Kant's categorical imperative, arguing that acting only in accordance with a maxim through which you can at the same time will that it become a universal law would allow 'outrageously immoral rules of conduct' to be adopted. However, that is only one formulation of the categorical imperative. Another is to so act as to use humanity, whether in one's own person or another's, always as an end, never merely as a means. While consequences, and what promotes or diminishes happiness, in particular, are important elements in moral decisions (and Kant can be criticized for ruling out consideration of consequences), is it not because we value human beings, and consider them to be ends in themselves, that we consider it important to try to satisfy human needs, and, indeed, to promote the happiness of other human beings?

Some Issues to Consider

- Mill grades pleasures, and argues that intellectual pleasures are more worthwhile than non-intellectual ones, but how helpful is this distinction when it comes to making actual moral decisions?
- Even if we accept that happiness is the only thing that people desire as an end, Mill does not give convincing reasons why we should be as concerned to promote other people's as our own. Concern for other people's happiness seems to presuppose attaching a value to them, and regarding them as ends in themselves.
- Mill's discussion of the relationship between utilitarianism and God's purpose for his creatures seems superficial, and to show lack of understanding of Christian teaching.
- Mill advocates the use of secondary moral principles, which would result in performing actions that will not create most happiness in a particular situation.

- Mill does not seem to have been attempting a strict proof of utilitarianism, so Moore's criticisms are not relevant to Mill's argument in *Utilitarianism*. However, Mill does not provide convincing reasons for accepting his view that happiness is the only thing that people desire as an end, or that the principle of utility is the sole criterion of morality.
- Mill's treatment of virtue and justice seem inadequate. Are these related to/based on utility, as he claims?

Suggestions for Further Reading

John Stuart Mill, *Autobiography*, ed. J. M. Robson, London: Penguin, 1989.

John Stuart Mill, *On Liberty and Other Essays*, ed. J. Gray, Oxford and New York: Oxford University Press, 1998.

John Stuart Mill, *Utilitarianism*, ed. G. Sher, 2nd edn, Indianapolis/Cambridge: Hackett Publishing Company, 2001.

R. Crisp, *Routledge Philosophy Guidebook to Mill on Utilitarianism*, London: Routledge, 1997.

Immanuel Kant, *Groundwork of the Metaphysics of Morals*, ed. M. Gregor, Cambridge: Cambridge University Press, 1998.

G. E. Moore, *Principia Ethica*, Amherst, NY: Prometheus Books, 1988.

W. Thomas, *John Stuart Mill*, Oxford and New York: Oxford University Press, 1985.

H. R. West, *An Introduction to Mill's Utilitarian Ethics*, Cambridge: Cambridge University Press, 2004.

Detailed Summary of John Stuart Mill's *Utilitarianism*

Chapter I (pp. 1–5)
General Remarks

It is surprising that so little progress has been made in deciding 'the **criterion of right and wrong**' (p. 1). The controversial question of the *summum bonum*, or the 'foundation of **morality**', has engaged the attention of the 'most gifted intellects' from the 'dawn of philosophy', but still there is no agreement (p. 1).

Similar 'uncertainty' surrounds the '**first principles**' of all sciences, including mathematics, but without impairing 'the trustworthiness' of their conclusions (p. 1). However, the explanation of this 'apparent anomaly' is that their operation does not depend on first principles, which, like the 'roots to a tree', function satisfactorily without being 'dug down to and exposed to light' (p. 2). But we expect the opposite in '**morals** or **legislation**'; as all 'action is for the sake of some **end**', the 'rules of action' will derive their character 'from the end to which they are subservient' (p. 2). So a '**test of right and wrong**' should be the means of deciding 'what is right or wrong', not 'a consequence' of having already done so (p. 2).

The problem is not solved by the 'popular theory' of a '**natural faculty**', telling us what is right or wrong (p. 2). The

9

existence of such a '**moral instinct**' is disputed, and even its advocates recognize that it could provide only the 'general **principles**' of morality, not specific **moral judgements**: judging the morality of an 'individual action' depends on applying 'a **law** to an individual case', not '**direct perception**' (p. 2). And when there is agreement about 'moral laws', differences exist about the 'source from which they derive their **authority**' (p. 2). Some consider them to be 'evident *a priori*', with obedience automatically following their meaning being understood; others hold that decisions about what is right or wrong are matters of '**observation and experience**' (pp. 2–3). Both schools of thought agree that 'morality must be **deduced** from principles', but they do not try to list the principles or 'reduce' them to 'one **first principle** or common ground of **obligation**' (p. 3). Instead, they assume the '*a priori* authority' of ordinary moral **precepts**, or offer, as their basis, 'some generality' less '**authoritative**' than the precepts themselves (p. 3). They need to provide either a 'fundamental' moral principle or an '**order of precedence**', in case the precepts conflict (p. 3).

It would be difficult to determine the 'bad effects' of the lack of an 'ultimate standard' of morality, but any 'consistency' in **moral beliefs** has been due to the 'tacit influence' on people's actual moral views of 'what they suppose to be the effects of things upon their **happiness**' (p. 3). This is the '**principle of utility**', which **Bentham** called, 'the **greatest happiness principle**'; and even those who deny that it is the fundamental moral principle acknowledge the importance of happiness in moral issues (p. 3). **Kant** laid down 'a universal first principle' ('So act that the rule on which thou actest would admit of being adopted as a law by all rational beings') as the basis of '**moral obligation**' (p. 4). However, his attempts to deduce actual **moral duties** from this principle showed no contradiction in rational beings adopting 'outrageously immoral rules of conduct', only the undesirable **consequences** of their doing so (p. 4).

I (says Mill) shall try to prove the 'utilitarian' or 'happiness' principle, as far as this can be done. However, '**ultimate ends** are not amenable to direct proof' (p. 4). Medical practice is proved to be good by the fact that it promotes health, but how can it be proved that 'health is good' (p. 4)? Music is good, because it affords **pleasure**, but what proof is there that 'pleasure is good' (p. 4)? Some things may be claimed to be good in themselves, while others are good 'as a **means**', not an end; but this cannot be proved in the ordinary sense (p. 4). Proof in morality means that the subject is one with which the '**rational faculty**' can deal on the basis of considerations that will determine the acceptance or rejection of a particular moral theory. However, an essential pre-condition of rational acceptance or rejection of the '**utilitarian formula**' is that it be understood, as lack of understanding is the 'chief obstacle' to its acceptance (p. 5). But before discussing the 'philosophical grounds' for accepting **utilitarianism**, I shall give some illustrations of it, to help remove the kind of objections that arise from 'mistaken interpretations' (p. 5).

Chapter II (pp. 6–26)
What Utilitarianism Is

A popular 'misconception', not held by utilitarianism's 'philosophical opponents', is that it is opposed to pleasure (p. 6). However, writers who have 'maintained the theory of utility', from **Epicurus** to Bentham, meant by it 'pleasure itself, together with exemption from **pain**' (p. 6). Utilitarianism considers actions 'right in proportion as they tend to promote happiness; wrong as they tend to produce the reverse'; that these are the 'only things desirable as ends'; and that things are desirable either for the 'pleasure **inherent**' in them, or their ability to promote pleasure or prevent pain (p. 7).

This theory arouses opposition; some consider it 'worthy only of swine' to believe that life possesses no '**nobler** object of **desire**' than pleasure (p. 7). But the Epicureans contended that a beast's pleasures do not meet human '**conceptions** of happiness', and that it was their opponents who thought human beings capable only of the pleasures of swine (p. 8). Like utilitarian writers in general, they recognized 'the superiority of mental over physical pleasures' (p. 8). Some pleasures are 'more desirable and more **valuable**' than others, and it would be absurd to think that **quantity** alone matters, and that **quality** should be ignored, only when we are estimating pleasure (p. 8).

But what makes one pleasure 'more valuable than another' (p. 8)? It is this: if, out of any two pleasures, there is one to which those who have experienced both 'give a decided preference', so that they would not swap it 'for any quantity of the other', that is the more desirable, due to **superior** quality (pp. 8–9). Further, there is no doubt that those who have experienced both much prefer pleasures which employ 'their **higher faculties**' (p. 9). Indeed, few humans would wish to be transformed into an animal, in exchange for 'the fullest allowance of a beast's pleasures' (p. 9). Unless extremely unhappy, no educated person would change places with a '**fool**' or a '**dunce**', just because they seemed satisfied with their lot (p. 9). A person possessing higher faculties may suffer because of them, but he would not choose a '**lower grade** of existence' (p. 9). We can explain this preference in various ways, including pride, but the most appropriate one is 'a sense of **dignity**'; and this is so 'essential' to the happiness of 'those in whom it is strong' that they would not desire anything that conflicted with it (p. 9). Of course, a person with limited 'capacities of enjoyment' is easily satisfied, while 'a highly endowed being' will always be aware of the world's 'imperfections' (p. 10). However, the latter will still be happier, because it is 'better to be a human being dissatisfied than a pig satisfied; better to be **Socrates** dissatisfied than a fool satisfied' (p. 10). And if the fool or the pig thinks differently, it is because 'they only know their side of the question' (p. 10).

But why do people, capable of '**higher pleasures**', sometimes opt for **lower** ones (p. 10)? It is because, through weakness, they may choose the '**nearer good**', though knowing it to be 'less valuable' (p. 10). We must also recognize that people may destroy their capacity for 'nobler feelings' through '**sensual indulgences**', or their capacity for nobler feelings may wither away, as a result of unfavourable circumstances, or failure to exercise them (p. 10). It is not that such people prefer '**inferior** pleasures' to higher ones; rather, it is only the inferior ones to which 'they have access', or which they are still 'capable of enjoying' (pp. 10–11).

So, on the question of which is the better of two pleasures or ways of life, the judgement of those who know both must be 'admitted as final' (p. 11). And we need not hesitate to accept such judgements about the quality of pleasures when we consider that there is no other 'tribunal' even on the question of quantity (p. 11). How can we decide which is the more acute of two pains, or the more intense of two pleasures, except by asking those familiar with both? We must accept the judgement that pleasures associated with the higher faculties are 'preferable *in kind*' to those connected with our '**animal nature**' (p. 11).

I have emphasized this point to give a 'just **conception** of utility or happiness considered as the **directive rule** of human conduct' (p. 11). However, it is not essential to acceptance of the '**utilitarian standard**', which is not the **agent**'s 'greatest happiness', but 'the greatest amount' altogether (p. 11). So, the 'ultimate end', to and for which everything else is desirable, is an existence as far as possible 'exempt' from pain and 'rich' in enjoyments, 'both in point of quantity and quality' (p. 12). And those best qualified to judge will decide the 'test' of the latter, and the 'rule' for measuring it against quantity (p. 12). And, as this is the 'end of human action', it is also 'the **standard of morality**' (p. 12).

But some argue that happiness is 'unattainable'; that we have no right to be happy anyway; or that human beings can manage without happiness (p. 12). The first would be a serious objection, but it applies only if happiness means 'a state of exalted pleasure', which will, of course, be transient (p. 13). However, we are talking about life that contains, in addition to such moments, little pain and a variety of pleasures. Many already experience such a life, and only poor **education** and bad **social arrangements** prevent it being available to almost all. But would the majority be satisfied with 'such a moderate share' of happiness (p. 13)? Well, the 'main constituents of a satisfied life' appear to be 'tranquillity and excitement': with the former, a little pleasure suffices, while the latter can reconcile people to much pain (p. 13). It seems possible to enable 'the mass of mankind to unite both' (p. 13). And when people, in 'tolerably fortunate' circumstances, do not find enough in life to make it 'valuable', it is usually because they care only for themselves (pp. 13–14). Those with 'objects of personal affection', particularly if they identify with 'the **collective interests of mankind**', remain interested in life into old age (p. 14).

A '**cultivated mind**' finds interest in all that surrounds it: in nature, art, poetry, history and so on (p. 14). And it is possible for every citizen of 'a civilized country' to achieve such a level of 'mental culture' (p. 14). In such an interesting world, all can develop at least 'genuine **private affections**' and a 'sincere interest in the **public good**': provided they have liberty and do not suffer from poverty or disease (p. 14). What is more, most of the 'great positive evils of the world' can be, and are being, removed (p. 15). There will be '**vicissitudes** of fortune', but these tend to be the result of 'imprudence', 'ill-regulated desires' or 'imperfect social institutions' (p. 15).

Thus, we can form a true estimate of the argument that we must learn 'to do without happiness' (p. 15). Yes, it is possible to do so; many are doing so; and heroes and martyrs choose to do so. But why do the latter choose to sacrifice 'their own portion of happiness' (p. 16)? We are told that their 'end is not happiness but **virtue**' (p. 16). However, would they make such sacrifices if they thought that they would not benefit their 'fellow creatures' (p. 16)? Indeed, although it shows the 'imperfect state' of the world, a person's readiness to serve others' happiness, by sacrificing his own, 'is the highest virtue which can be found in man'; and utilitarian morality acknowledges human beings' power to sacrifice 'their own greatest good for the good of others' (p. 16). However, it denies that such sacrifice is good in itself, because it is a waste unless it increases 'the sum total of happiness' (p. 17).

Opponents seldom acknowledge that utilitarianism requires the agent to be '**impartial**' between his own and other people's happiness: **Jesus' golden rule**, 'do as you would be done by', and the teaching, 'love your neighbour as yourself', constitute 'the ideal perfection of utilitarian morality' (p. 17). Thus, 'laws and social arrangements' should place individual happiness 'in harmony with the interest of the whole', while education and **public opinion** should ensure that individual happiness and 'the **general good**' are firmly linked (p. 17). A desire to promote the latter should be everyone's priority.

But critics do not always place utilitarianism in a 'discreditable light' (p. 18). Some say that it is too 'exacting' to ask human beings always to promote 'the general interests of society'; but this mistakes 'the rule of action' with its motive (p. 18). The job of **ethics** is 'to tell us what are our **duties**', but this does not mean that 'a feeling of **duty**' motivates all that we do (p. 18). In most things, we rightly act from other motives. And this criticism is particularly unfair to utilitarianism, which teaches that 'motive has nothing to do with the morality of the action' (p. 18). Saving someone from drowning is morally right, irrespective of motive. Further, it is a 'misapprehension' that utilitarianism requires people always to focus on 'society at large' (p. 19). Most good actions are intended to benefit individuals. While 'multiplication of happiness' is the 'object of virtue', few opportunities exist to do so on 'an extended scale', so most of us are concerned with the happiness of a few (p. 19). There are also 'abstinences', where we refrain from actions which, though possibly beneficial in specific cases, belong to a 'class' that is 'generally injurious' (p. 19).

Another objection to utilitarianism is that it makes its followers 'cold and unsympathizing', as they concentrate on 'the consequences of actions' and ignore the human qualities from which actions flow (p. 20). But no '**ethical standard**' deems an action right or wrong on the basis of the agent's personal qualities (p. 20). Further, a right action does not necessarily signify 'a virtuous character' (p. 20). Preoccupation with measuring 'the morality of actions' by 'utilitarian standards' may lead some utilitarians to neglect 'other beauties' of human character, but, in fact, utilitarians vary in the rigidity with which they apply their standard (p. 21). Utilitarianism's great merit is that it provides a 'tangible and intelligible mode' of deciding moral questions (p. 21).

Utilitarianism has been called a *'godless* doctrine': but, if **God**'s purpose in creation is his creatures' happiness, it is 'profoundly religious' (pp. 21–2). The objection may mean that utilitarianism does not take 'the **revealed will of God** as the **supreme law** of morals' (p. 22). Well, a utilitarian who thinks that God is **perfectly good** necessarily believes that God's revelation about morality must meet 'the requirements of utility' (p. 22). However, it is not only utilitarians who believe that the intention of '**Christian** revelation' was to help human beings to discover for themselves what is right (p. 22). Anyway, the aid of **religion** is as available to the 'utilitarian **moralist**' as to any other (p. 22).

Utilitarianism is 'stigmatized' as immoral and **expedient** (p. 22). But 'expedient', in the sense in which it is 'opposed to the right', generally refers to that which benefits the agent, or which assists achievement of 'some immediate object', while breaking a rule that is 'expedient in a much higher degree' (p. 22). In these cases, it means 'hurtful', not 'useful' (p. 22). An example would be lying, which might be expedient to get out of a particular difficulty, but weakens the 'trustworthiness of human assertion' that underpins 'social well-being' (p. 23). There may be legitimate exceptions, as when withholding bad news from an extremely ill person; but these need to be 'defined' (p. 23).

Again, utilitarians are told that, in any given situation, it would be impossible to calculate 'the effects of any line of conduct on the **general happiness**' (p. 23). This is like suggesting that Christianity cannot guide our actions, because there would not be time to read through the **Old and New Testaments**. But there has been 'the whole past duration of the human species', during which **experience** will have shown 'the tendencies of actions' (p. 23). Some people talk as if we are only now starting to consider the harm caused to 'human happiness' by murder and theft (p. 24). Yes, rules of morality are 'improvable', but it would be 'universal idiocy' to ignore past experience, and to try 'to test each individual action directly by the first principle' (p. 24). It is a 'strange notion' to hold that acceptance of a first principle is inconsistent with acknowledgement of '**secondary** ones' (p. 24). Proposing happiness as 'the end and aim of morality' does not mean that people journeying there cannot be advised about the road to take (p. 24). Whatever '**fundamental principle** of morality' we adopt, we need '**subordinate** principles' by which to apply it (p. 25).

Utilitarians are also accused of an inclination to make themselves exceptions to moral rules, as if such a tendency is unique to them. However, all ethical creeds do allow for exceptions, 'under the moral responsibility of the agent', and accept the existence of 'cases of conflicting obligation' (p. 25). But at least utilitarianism provides an 'ultimate standard' to decide between 'incompatible' demands; and it is only when secondary principles conflict that 'first principles should be appealed to' (p. 26).

Chapter III (pp. 27–34)
Of the Ultimate Sanction of the Principle of Utility

Why should we obey a particular '**moral standard**' (p. 27)? What is the 'source of its obligation' (p. 27)? **Moral philosophy** must answer this question, which arises 'whenever a person is called on to *adopt* a standard' (p. 27). Only '**customary morality**' feels '*in itself* obligatory', so it seems strange when it is asserted that it *'derives'* its obligation from some general principle', which lacks the same 'halo' of custom (p. 27). People think that they are 'bound' not to murder, rob or deceive, but they do not feel bound to promote the general happiness (p. 27).

If utilitarian theories about the 'moral sense' are right, this difficulty will persist until the 'influences which form moral character' have grasped the principle of utility to the same extent that they have grasped the consequences of it (p. 27). The sense of 'unity with our fellow creatures' needs to be as ingrained in our nature as 'Christ intended' (p. 27). For the time being, utilitarianism shares this problem with other moral systems.

All the internal and external **sanctions** of other moral systems are available to utilitarianism. External sanctions consist of the approval or condemnation of our 'fellow creatures' and God (p. 28). Certainly, it is the case that people desire happiness, and approve of conduct in others that promotes their own happiness, while believers in God's goodness must also think that he approves that which is conducive to happiness. As for internal sanctions, duty is 'a feeling in our own mind', which can make us shrink from some actions as 'an impossibility' (p. 28). This is 'the essence of **conscience**', which can impart a '**mystical** character . . . to the idea of moral obligation' (p. 29). And if, apart from external ones, the ultimate sanction of morality is these 'conscientious feelings', there is no reason why they should not support utilitarianism as strongly as 'any other rule of morals' (p. 29).

Now some hold that people are more likely to accept moral obligation if they regard it as a '**transcendental** fact' (p. 29). But even if a person believes in God, he is urged to moral action by 'his own **subjective** feeling' (p. 30). Belief in God only affects his conduct in proportion to the strength of his 'religious feeling' (p. 30). However, '**transcendental moralists**' seem to believe that the internal sanction of conscience will only be effective, if it has 'its root out of the mind' (p. 30). They fear that if it is seen as merely a feeling, people may 'disregard' it when it proves 'inconvenient' (p. 30). However, this is not a problem only for utilitarians; people's willingness to ignore their conscience is a cause of concern to 'all moralists' (p. 30).

Also, there is no need to decide whether 'the feeling of duty is **innate** or **implanted**' (p. 30). Even those who believe it to be innate accept that '**intuitive** perception' is of the principles, not the details, of morality (p. 30). But, if there is an innate element, it could just as well be 'regard to the pleasures and pains of others' as anything else (p. 30). Indeed, 'intuitive moralists' agree that a large part of morality concerns consideration for the 'interests of our fellow creatures' (pp. 30–1). My own view is that 'moral feelings' are not innate, but that the 'moral faculty' is a 'natural outgrowth' from our nature, capable of limited spontaneous development, but requiring careful cultivation (p. 31). Sadly, it is capable 'of being cultivated in almost any direction', so that 'absurd' and 'mischievous' principles can acquire 'all the authority of conscience' (p. 31).

Of course, moral beliefs, however strongly held, can be dissolved away by analysis: unless there is something in our nature with which they 'harmonize' (p. 31). In the case of 'utilitarian morality', promoting the 'general happiness' harmonizes with the 'social feelings of mankind': our desire 'to be in unity with our fellow creatures' (pp. 31–2). Indeed, an essential condition of any 'state of society' is that the interests of all its members are consulted (p. 32). There can be no society of equals, unless 'the interests of all are to be regarded equally' (p. 32). As society has developed, we have become more accustomed to 'co-operating with others', and this fosters the sense of others' interests being our own (p. 32). Thus, the 'good of others' becomes something to which we 'naturally and neces-sarily' attend (p. 33). Further, political reform, by eliminating legal and other 'inequalities' between individuals, increases the influences that produce in them 'a feeling of unity' with other people (p. 33). And, if this feeling were to become 'perfect', it would be impossible for individuals to desire bene-fits which others would not share (p. 33). If we imagine all society's resources being used to teach this feeling of unity 'as a religion', we can see that there need be no doubts about 'the sufficiency of the ultimate sanction for the happiness morality' (p. 33).

And, even in society's present imperfect state, 'social feel-ing' makes it difficult to regard others merely as 'struggling rivals . . . for the means of happiness' (p. 34). We feel that there should be 'harmony' between our own 'feelings and aims' and those of our 'fellow creatures' (p. 34). In most people, this feeling may, as yet, be less powerful than 'their selfish feel-ings'; and in some it is lacking altogether (p. 34). But there are few, apart from those 'whose mind is a moral blank', who would wish to lead their lives 'on the plan of paying no regard to others' (p. 34).

Chapter IV (pp. 35–41)
Of What Sort of Proof the Principle of Utility is Susceptible

As previously mentioned, 'ultimate ends' are not provable in the ordinary sense (p. 35). In fact, no first principles, whether of knowledge or conduct, can be proved 'by reasoning' (p. 35). However, the former, as 'matters of fact', can be judged by our **faculties** (p. 35). But what about morality? What will persuade people to accept the 'utilitarian doctrine' that happiness is both desirable and 'the only thing desirable, as an end' (p. 35)?

Well, the only proof of the visibility of an object is that 'people actually see it' (p. 35). Similarly, the only possible evidence of something's desirability is that 'people do actually desire it' (p. 35). No reason can be given for the desirability of the general happiness, except that each individual 'desires his own happiness' (p. 35). But here we have all the proof that is possible or required: 'each person's happiness is a good to that person, and the general happiness, therefore, a good to the aggregate of all persons' (pp. 35–6). So, happiness is both an end of conduct and 'one of the criteria of morality' (p. 36). But can it be the 'sole criterion' (p. 36)? This would require it to be the only thing people desire; but people clearly desire things, 'distinguished from happiness', such as virtue (p. 36). Thus, utilitarianism's opponents feel entitled to claim that, as 'human action' seeks other ends, happiness is not the only standard of morality (p. 36).

But there is no conflict here. While utilitarian moralists believe that actions are only virtuous to the extent that they 'promote another end', granted acceptance of that end, they put virtue at the top of things that are 'good as a means to the ultimate end' (p. 36). And they recognize the 'psychological' importance of its being 'a good in itself' (p. 36). We must remember, too, that the 'ingredients of happiness' are both 'various' and desirable in themselves (p. 36). So, we must not regard, for example, health as just a means to 'a collective something termed happiness' (pp. 36–7). It is 'desired and desirable' in itself, and is 'part of the end' (p. 37). And virtue can also become 'a part' of happiness (p. 37).

This point can be illustrated further. Virtue is not the only means which, 'by association with what it is a means to', comes to be 'desired for itself' (p. 37). Money is desired, not just as a means to happiness, but for itself, as part of the end of happiness. The same is true of power and fame. What were once desired as means to 'attainment of happiness' are now desired for their own sake, 'as *part* of happiness' (p. 37). And this is sanctioned by utilitarianism, because happiness is not 'an abstract idea but a concrete whole; and these are some of its parts' (p. 38).

According to utilitarianism, the original value of virtue lies in its 'conduciveness' to promoting pleasure and preventing pain (p. 38). But, through association with these ends, it has come to be seen as 'a good in itself' (p. 38). Further, it has this advantage over the desire for money, power or fame: it does not make the individual '**noxious**' to others (p. 38). So, while utilitarianism tolerates the other desires up to the point at which they start to damage, rather than promote, general happiness, it encourages cultivation of a love of virtue 'up to the greatest strength possible' (p. 38).

Therefore, nothing is desired except happiness. Other things, such as virtue, are desired as a means to happiness, or because they are part of happiness. And we can now answer the question about what proof we can give for 'the principle of utility' (p. 39). If human beings desire only things that are part of, or a means to, happiness, it is 'the sole end of human action' (p. 39). Thus, promoting happiness is the test for judging human conduct, so 'it must be the criterion of morality' (p. 39).

But do people actually 'desire nothing for itself but that which is a pleasure to them, or of which the absence is a pain' (p. 39)? This can only be decided by 'self-observation, assisted by observation of others'; but it will 'hardly be disputed' (p. 39). The only objection will be that the 'will is a different thing from desire', and that virtuous people carry out their purposes without thinking of the pleasure to be derived from them (p. 39). However, this is to do with 'the power of habit', so that, instead of willing things that we desire, we often find ourselves desiring things because we will them (p. 40). But this is not confined to 'virtuous actions' (p. 40). There are many things that we once did from a motive, but now do from habit. However, originally the will is 'entirely produced by desire', including both pleasure and pain (p. 40). Therefore, if someone has a feeble 'virtuous will', we would strengthen it by making that person desire virtue, through associating doing right with pleasure and not doing so with pain (p. 40). However, this is not to diminish the importance of habit in acting rightly. The influence of 'pleasurable and painful associations' is not foolproof, whereas habit 'imparts certainty' (p. 41). Therefore, although nothing is 'a good to human beings', except what is 'pleasurable' in itself, or is 'a means of attaining pleasure or averting pain', we must cultivate into a habit 'the will to do right', so that others can depend upon our conduct (p. 41).

Chapter V (pp. 42–64)
On the Connection Between Justice and Utility

Justice has been one of the 'strongest obstacles' to accepting utility as the 'criterion of right and wrong', because it appears to be **'generically distinct'** from what is expedient; we believe that we have 'natural feelings of justice' (p. 42). But this does not necessarily mean that they must be acknowledged as 'an ultimate criterion of conduct' (p. 42). We tend to think that a 'subjective feeling' reveals an 'objective reality', and it is difficult to regard justice as only a 'particular kind' of 'general utility', because its 'superior binding force' seems to indicate 'a totally different origin' (p. 43). So, we need to determine whether an action's justice or injustice is 'intrinsically peculiar and distinct from all its other qualities', or just a particular combination of them (p. 43). Then we can identify 'the distinguishing character' of justice, and decide whether there is a quality that is common to all conduct deemed 'as just or as **unjust**' (p. 43)? If so, is there something in human nature that explains why it arouses such strong feelings, or is our response 'a special provision of nature' (p. 43)?

Let us start by reviewing the type of actions that we class as just or unjust.

First, it is generally considered unjust to deprive a person of such things as liberty or property, which belong to him 'by law' (p. 44). So, it is 'just to respect, unjust to violate' someone's **legal rights** (p. 44). Second, there are exceptions. A person may forfeit his rights, or the law conferring them may be a bad one. But opinions differ here. Some maintain that even bad laws should be obeyed, although it is permissible to campaign to change them. This approach is defended on grounds of expediency: society gains from the principle of 'submission to law' being upheld (p. 44). Others argue that unjust, or even inexpedient, laws may be disobeyed. But it certainly seems to be accepted that there may be unjust laws; that, therefore, law cannot be 'the ultimate criterion of justice'; and that unjust laws deprive people of a *'moral right'* (pp. 44–5).

Third, it is also generally held that justice involves a person receiving his deserts ('good if he does right, evil if he does wrong'), especially from those to whom he has done good or evil (p. 45). Fourth, it is unjust to *'break faith'* with a person. However, this can be 'overruled' if, for example, the person's conduct is held to 'absolve us from our obligation' (p. 45).

Fifth, being *'partial'* is inconsistent with justice (p. 45). It is unjust to favour one person over another in situations where it is inappropriate to do so. Clearly, favouring particular persons is not always inappropriate, as with 'family or friends', but doing so must not conflict with other duties (p. 45). In such areas as the law and selection for government office, impartiality means being influenced only by the considerations which 'ought to influence the particular case in hand' (p. 46). Linked to impartiality is the idea of '*equality*' (p. 46). But there are difficulties with it. People tend to argue that justice demands equality, except where 'expediency requires inequality' (p. 46). They may urge 'equal protection' of the rights of all, while defending 'inequality in the rights themselves' (p. 46). Thus, in 'slave countries', there may be insistence on upholding the rights of slaves as well as masters, but the institutions that deny rights to the slaves are not deemed unjust, because they are expedient (p. 46). Again, those who believe in government see no injustice in the inequality involved in granting to magistrates powers 'not granted to other people' (p. 46).

With so many 'applications of the term "justice"', it is hard to find the 'mental link' holding them together (p. 47). Perhaps etymology will help. This points to an origin connected with law: 'the primitive element' in forming the idea of justice was 'conformity to law' (p. 47). Among some ancient peoples, this did not rule out the possibility of bad laws, so the idea of injustice was attached, 'not to all violations of law, but only to violations of such laws as *ought* to exist' (p. 47). Thus, 'the idea of law' remained 'predominant' in the idea of justice, even if actual laws were not regarded as 'the standard of it' (p. 48).

Human beings, of course, consider that justice applies to many things that are not, and which no one wishes to be, 'regulated by law' (p. 48). For example, we recognize that people behave justly or unjustly in 'private life' (p. 48). But, although we might like to see 'just conduct enforced', even in this area, we are unwilling to entrust the 'magistrate with so unlimited an amount of power over individuals' (p. 48).

But what distinguishes the obligations associated with justice from 'moral obligation in general' (p. 48)? For the idea of 'penal sanction . . . the essence of law, enters not only into the conception of injustice, but into that of any kind of wrong' (p. 48). When we call something wrong, we suggest that the person who did it should be punished. Here is the difference between 'morality and simple expediency' (p. 49). The idea of duty includes the idea of people being 'compelled to fulfill it', because it can be '*exacted*' from them (p. 49). We might wish people to do, or not do, certain things, but we recognize that there are cases where moral obligation does not apply, and in which punishment would be inappropriate.

But what 'distinguishes justice from other branches of morality' (p. 49)? We can divide duties into those of '**perfect** and of **imperfect obligation**' (p. 49). The former are those 'in virtue of which a correlative right resides in some person or persons'; the latter 'do not give birth to any right' (pp. 49–50). Now, 'this distinction exactly coincides with that . . . between justice and the other obligations of morality' (p. 50). Justice (unlike, for example, generosity, which is not due to any 'given individual') implies, not only something that it is right or wrong to do or not do, but also something which a given 'person can claim from us as his moral right' (p. 50). And, unless we make this distinction between 'justice and morality in general', we end up merging 'all morality in justice' (p. 50).

We are now in a position to decide whether the feeling that accompanies justice attaches to it by a 'special dispensation of nature', or could have grown 'out of the idea itself' (p. 51). And it seems to me that the 'essential ingredients' in the idea of justice are the desire to punish the person who has done harm, and the belief that there is a 'definite individual' who has been harmed (p. 51). It also seems that the desire to punish arises from two natural sentiments: 'the impulse of self-defense and the feeling of sympathy' (p. 51). The first is 'common to all animal nature', but, due to 'superior intelligence', human beings are conscious of a common interest with other people, bringing out the 'instinct . . . of self-defense', if their community is threatened (p. 51). And this corresponds to the 'desire to punish' in the sentiment of justice, which is only moral in that it is directed towards the 'general good' (p. 52).

It is true that, when our sense of justice is outraged, we may be thinking of a specific case, affecting us, rather than 'society at large' (p. 52). But we feel that we are 'asserting a rule which is for the benefit of others' in society as well as ourselves (p. 52). If we are concerned with the act only as it affects us, we fail to be 'consciously just' (p. 52). Even 'anti-utilitarian moralists' admit this (p. 52). Kant's previously referred to fundamental principle of morals 'virtually acknowledges' that 'the interest of mankind collectively' must be in the agent's mind when he conscientiously decides on 'the morality of the act' (p. 52). Clearly, it is not the case that an utterly selfish rule 'could not *possibly* be adopted by all rational beings' (p. 52). Therefore, Kant's principle must mean that our conduct ought to be shaped by a rule, 'which all rational beings might adopt *with benefit to their collective interest*' (p. 53).

So, the idea of justice 'supposes two things': a rule of conduct, which must be 'common to all mankind and intended for their good', and a sentiment, sanctioning the rule, which is the desire that those who infringe the rule be punished (p. 53). Further, it involves a definite person, 'whose rights . . . are violated' by the infringement (p. 53). And, by a 'person's

right', we mean that he has a 'valid claim on society to protect him in possession of it', either by law or public opinion
(p. 53). For example, a person has a right to what he can earn
in 'fair professional competition'; society ought not to allow
others to stop him doing so (p. 53). But he does not have a right
to £300 a year, as society is not required to guarantee him a
particular sum. And the only reason I can give as to why society should protect people's rights is 'general utility': to give all
of us the 'security', upon which 'all our immunity from evil'
and 'the whole value of all and every good' depends (p. 54).
And this security is so important that our claim on our 'fellow
creatures', to co-operate with us in ensuring it, assumes the
'character of absoluteness' (p. 54).

Now, if this analysis of justice is wrong, and it is 'totally
independent of utility' and a 'standard *per se*', why do so many
things appear just or unjust 'according to the light in which
they are regarded' (p. 55)? It is alleged that 'utility is an uncer-
tain standard', subject to various interpretations, whereas
there can be no 'doubt' about justice (p. 55). In fact, there is as
much 'difference of opinion' about 'what is just as about what
is useful' (p. 55).

Some argue that it is unjust to punish people as 'an example
to others'; some that it is wrong to punish people 'for their own
benefit'; others that it is 'unjust to punish at all', as criminals
do not make their character (p. 55). So how do we settle such
differences? Various 'devices' have been invented (p. 56). There
is 'freedom of the will': it is unjust to punish a person whose
will is in a 'hateful state', unless there are no outside factors
that have caused it to be so (p. 56). Then there is the 'fiction of
a contract' (p. 56). In the past, 'members of society' agreed to
obey laws, empowering legislators to punish disobedience, for
their own or society's good (p. 56).

Indeed, accepting the legitimacy of inflicting punishment, look at all the different ideas of justice that there are on the subject of 'the proper apportionment of punishments to offenses' (p. 57). There is still a 'secret hankering' after the '*lex talionis*, an eye for an eye and a tooth for a tooth' (p. 57). For many, the 'test of justice' is that punishment is 'proportioned to the offense', and is determined by the 'moral guilt' of the offender, irrespective of considerations of deterrence (p. 57). For others, the opposite is the case: it is unacceptable to impose a greater degree of punishment than is necessary to prevent repetition of the crime.

Let us look at an example from a different area. In industry, is it just that those with greater skills receive 'superior remuneration' (p. 57)? Some argue that, provided people do their best, their lack of skill should not be penalized; those with superior skill already enjoy great advantages without being given a greater 'share of the world's goods' (p. 57). Others contend that, as efficient workers contribute more to society, they deserve more (pp. 57–8). How do we decide between these two 'conflicting principles of justice' (p. 58)?

Is it just for taxation to be 'graduated', taking more from those who have more (p. 58)? But why not require the same sum from all, as all receive the same 'protection . . . of law and government' (p. 58). In the shops, prices do not vary according to the means of the customer. People argue that the state 'does more for the rich', to justify the higher taxes they pay (p. 58). But this is not so. In the absence of law and government, the rich would be better equipped to defend themselves, and might succeed in 'converting the poor into their slaves' (pp. 58–9).

The idea of justice gives rise to much confusion. Is, therefore, the difference between the just and the expedient 'merely imaginary' (p. 59)? No, there is 'a real distinction' (p. 59). While I reject any theory that seeks to set up 'an imaginary standard of justice not grounded on utility', justice that is so grounded is 'the chief' and 'most sacred' part of morality (p. 59). It refers to a class of moral rules that 'concern the essentials of human well-being', and these impose 'more absolute obligation' than any others (p. 59). And the 'essence of the idea of justice' lies in the rights 'residing in an individual' (p. 59).

The moral rules forbidding human beings 'to hurt one another', which include respect for other people's freedom, matter more to 'human well-being' than any others (p. 59). It is through observing them that 'peace among human beings' is preserved (p. 59). A person may not need the help of others, 'but he always needs that they should not do him hurt' (p. 60). Thus, the 'moralities' protecting individuals against harm from others are the ones which we have 'the strongest interest in publishing and enforcing', and which primarily 'compose the obligation of justice' (p. 60). The most significant 'cases of injustice' are 'wrongful aggression or wrongful exercise of power' over a person, followed by withholding from a person 'something which is his due' (p. 60).

The motives that require 'observance of these primary moralities' also demand the punishment of those who breach them (p. 60). Giving 'evil for evil' is included in the idea of justice, but so, too, is giving good for good; if we accept benefits, we should give 'a return of them' (p. 60). Thus, the principle of 'giving to each what they deserve', both good for good and evil for evil, is not only included in the idea of justice, but is 'a proper object of that intensity of sentiment which places the just . . . above the simply expedient' (p. 61).

Most 'maxims of justice', such as a person being responsible only for what he has done voluntarily, that it is unjust to condemn someone unheard, and proportioning the punishment to the crime, are just means, drawn from 'the practice' of the law courts, of ensuring that 'the just principle of evil for evil' is not perverted into inflicting evil without that justification (p. 61). Take the 'maxims of impartiality and equality' (p. 61). If it is a duty to 'do to each according to his deserts', society must 'treat all equally well' (pp. 61–2). And this 'great moral duty' flows from 'the first principle of morals'; the principle of utility is a 'mere form of words', unless one person's happiness counts 'for exactly as much as another's' (p. 62). Everybody's equal claim to happiness involves 'an equal claim to all the means of happiness', to the extent that the conditions of life and the 'general interest' permit (pp. 62–3). Everybody is considered to have a '*right* to equality of treatment, except when some recognized social expediency requires the reverse' (p. 63). Thus, 'social inequalities', such as the distinction between slaves and freemen, or nobles and serfs, which are no longer thought expedient, come to be seen as unjust (p. 63). People wonder why they were ever tolerated; and so it will be with 'color, race and sex' (p. 63).

It seems that justice indicates those 'moral requirements' that are higher in 'the scale of social utility' than others, and carry 'paramount obligation': although there will be occasions, such as needing to seize the means of saving a life, when 'the general maxims of justice' are overruled (pp. 63–4). In these situations, we tend to say, not that justice must 'give way to some other moral principle', but that what is generally just is not so in this particular case (p. 64).

It has always been clear that 'all cases of justice are also cases of expediency', with the difference of the 'peculiar sentiment' attaching to the former (p. 64). However, if the above explains all this, the idea of justice will no longer be 'a stumbling block to the utilitarian ethics' (p. 64). Justice is the name for 'certain social utilities', which matter more than others, and which are rightly supported by a more powerful sentiment than that attached 'to the mere idea of promoting human pleasure' (p. 64).

Overview

Chapter I (General Remarks, pp. 1–5)

Mill maintains that, despite the interest taken in the question of right and wrong, little progress has been made in establishing the foundation of morality. Indeed, there are many views, which include belief in a moral instinct and the conflicting theories that moral principles are evident *a priori*, or that they should be based on observation and experience. Such consistency as there has been in moral beliefs has been due to the influence of the principle of utility or the greatest happiness principle. *Utilitarianism* is an attempt to prove that this principle is the foundation of morality, but in the context of recognition that ordinary standards of proof cannot be achieved in this area.

Chapter II (What Utilitarianism Is, pp. 6–26)

Mill explains that utilitarianism is the theory that actions should be judged by the principle of utility: they are right to the extent that they promote pleasure and happiness, and wrong to the extent that they promote pain. This is a matter of quality as much as quantity, because some pleasures are more valuable than others. Mill argues that the more worthwhile of any two pleasures is the one chosen by people with experience of both, and that intellectual pleasures, enjoyed by educated people, have a higher value than purely physical ones. People who enjoy intellectual pleasures may also be conscious of life's imperfections, while those who do not may be easily satisfied, but the former would not wish to change places with the latter. It is preferable to be Socrates dissatisfied than a fool satisfied.

Mill stresses the point that utilitarianism is not concerned exclusively with the agent's own happiness, but with general happiness. It requires the agent to be impartial between his own and other people's happiness, and people must try to apply Jesus' golden rule to their relations with others. He deals with various objections to utilitarianism. The view that happiness is unattainable reflects a misunderstanding of what utilitarians mean by it. Happiness is not a permanent state of pleasure, but a well-balanced way of life, characterized by a variety of pleasures, such as intellectual pursuits, family relationships and friendship, and engagement with the concerns of society, and which contains little pain.

It is thought unreasonable to expect people always to promote general happiness, but Mill explains that they are not expected to do so. For most people, their opportunities to perform good actions relate to just a few others. Nor is utilitarianism a godless doctrine, because it fits in with God's purpose, if that purpose is his creatures' happiness. Another objection is the impossibility of calculating the effects of particular actions on general happiness, but this does not have to be done every time an action is contemplated. Use can be made of accepted rules of morality, such as those concerning murder and theft. These reflect humanity's experience of the kind of actions that harm human happiness, and which need to be prohibited. However, the principle of utility can be invoked when these subordinate principles conflict.

Chapter III (Of the Ultimate Sanction of the Principle of Utility, pp. 27–34)

Mills considers utilitarianism's source of obligation. Unlike customary morality, the principle of utility lacks the sense of being obligatory, and this will continue until it achieves general acceptance. However, all the sanctions available to other moral systems are available to it, including (as it gains acceptance) public opinion and the influence of conscience. Mill does not think that moral feelings are innate, but, whether they are innate or implanted, there is no reason why they should not include consideration for the pleasures and pains of others.

He recognizes that moral beliefs can be dissolved away by analysis, but maintains that concern for the good of others, and promotion of general happiness, harmonize with the obligations we naturally feel towards other members of society. This concern for the interests of all is an essential element in the existence and development of society, which needs to devote resources to cultivating it.

Chapter IV (Of What Sort of Proof the Principle of Utility is Susceptible, pp. 35–41)

Mill has already acknowledged the difficulty of proving a fundamental moral principle, but he is searching for a means of persuading people to accept the utilitarian view that happiness is both desirable and the only thing that is desirable as an end. He draws an analogy with visibility. The only proof that things are visible is that people see them, so the only possible evidence that something is desirable is that people actually desire it: each person's happiness is a good to that person, and the general good to the aggregate of all persons. Happiness is, therefore, both an end of human conduct and a criterion by which we judge morality.

Mill tackles the question of whether it is the only thing people desire as an end and the sole criterion of morality, given people's apparent desire for things other than happiness, such as virtue. He denies the existence of any real conflict. Happiness is the ultimate end, but other things are good *in so far* as they are a means to that end. However, there is psychological value in their being regarded as good in themselves, while some things, like virtue, are so closely associated with happiness that they become part of the end, and thus part of happiness. Mill concludes that if human beings desire only things that are a part of, or a means to happiness, it is the sole end of human action, while promoting happiness is the test for judging human conduct, and the sole criterion of morality. He suggests that people observe themselves and others to see whether or not he is right.

Chapter V (Of the Connection Between Justice and Utility, pp. 42–64)

Mill deals with the issue of whether justice, which seems to be generically distinct from the principle of utility, and to have a binding force, can in fact be reconciled with acceptance of the latter as the criterion of right and wrong. He examines the types of action that are generally classed as just and unjust. Unjust actions include depriving people of things, such as liberty and property, which belong to them by law, breaking faith, and showing people favour in situations, such as appointments to government posts, where it is inappropriate to do so. It is difficult to decide what links the different applications of justice together, or what distinguishes obligations associated with justice from moral obligation in general, in view of the fact that both involve the idea of duties that people should fulfil and of their being punished for failing to do so.

He decides that what distinguishes justice from other forms of moral obligation is that, unlike generosity, for example, which is an imperfect obligation, and is not owed to any particular person, justice involves perfect obligation, because there is something that a particular person can claim from us as his moral right. He concludes that justice involves a rule of conduct, which must be common to all human beings, and which is intended for their good; a desire for the punishment of those who break the rule; and a particular person whose rights have been violated, and who has a valid claim on society (whether through law or public opinion) to uphold those rights. And the only reason why society should protect the rights of others is utility: to give all members of society that security without which nothing can be enjoyed. Indeed, such security is so important that every member of society has an absolute obligation to co-operate in ensuring it.

Mill considers that the correctness of his analysis of justice is borne out by the fact that the same things appear just or unjust, depending upon the standpoint from which they are considered. He illustrates his argument by reference to the wide range of views on the justice of punishing people for their crimes.

However, although justice is grounded on utility, Mill does not believe that there is no difference between what is just and what is expedient: justice, when based on utility, is the most important part of morality. This is because it is concerned with the essentials of human well-being, such as the rules forbidding people to hurt each other and those guaranteeing individual freedom. Therefore justice indicates moral requirements that are higher in the scale of social utility, and which matter more, than others; therefore, enforcing them must be a high priority for society.

Glossary

Act utilitarianism. Utilitarianism which requires reference to the principle of utility every time an act is contemplated, to determine the amount of happiness it will promote, compared to other possible actions. Bentham developed the felicific calculus, to calculate the quantities of pleasure (and/or) pain that different possible actions will produce. The advantage is the focus on the happiness potential of individual actions; the disadvantages (as Mill observes) are that it ignores past experience, is time-consuming, and comes up against the difficulty of calculating all the possible consequences of a potential action.

Agent. One who performs an action.

Animal nature. Mill distinguishes between the lower pleasures, associated with human beings' animal nature/basic desires, and the higher pleasures, associated with the intellect.

A priori. That which comes before experience, and which holds (or is claimed to hold) irrespective of experience. Some believe that this is the case with moral principles: that they prescribe standards of conduct for human beings, irrespective of the human condition and general or individual needs.

Authoritative. Having authority.

Authority. Mill is concerned with the source from which moral systems and the principle of utility, in particular, derive their authority.

Bentham, Jeremy (1748–1832). The founder of utilitarianism and friend of both John Stuart Mill and his father, the philosopher, James Mill. Bentham sought to establish the greatest happiness principle as the accepted end of human action and the criterion of morality. However, unlike Mill, he was not interested in the distinction between higher and lower/more and less valuable pleasures.

Christianity. Mill discusses Christianity and its relationship to utilitarianism. See also God, godless, golden rule, Jesus.

Collective interests of mankind. People's common interests as members of society, which include security and freedom.

Conception. Idea (of).

Conscience. Human beings' awareness of what is right and wrong, which deters them from even contemplating such actions as theft or murder. Mill regarded conscience, not as a God-given faculty, but as a human capacity, capable of being developed to support undesirable as well as desirable moral principles/rules of conduct. Through education, conscience could be cultivated to support utilitarian principles.

Consequences. Results (of actions). Utilitarianism is concerned with the results of actions, and the extent to which they promote happiness. Hence it is a consequentialist moral system.

Consequentialist (of system of morals). One which decides whether an action is right or wrong on the basis of its consequences. Utilitarianism judges actions to be right to the extent that they promote pleasure and wrong to the extent that they promote pain. See also deontological (of system of morals).

Criterion of right and wrong/morality. A standard for deciding which actions are right and which are wrong. According to Mill, (that which promotes) happiness is the sole criterion of what is right or wrong.

Glossary

Cultivated mind. Educated mind, which has been educated to appreciate, and find pleasure in, intellectual pursuits.

Customary morality. Rules of right and wrong which people have been taught, which they accept (often without question), and which they feel bound to obey. Mill makes the point that people will need education, if they are to realize that such rules as those forbidding murder and theft rest ultimately on the principle of utility.

Deduce. Draw a conclusion from certain premises (propositions), from which it may follow necessarily: that is, acceptance of the premises, but denial of the conclusion, would involve a contradiction. Mill refers to the view of some moralists that rules of action can be can be deduced from certain *a priori* moral principles.

Deontological (of system of morals). One, such as Kant's, which treats certain actions as being right or wrong in themselves, irrespective of their consequences. Thus, a believer in a deontological moral system would say that it was always wrong to lie, even if, in a particular situation (for example, denying knowledge of the whereabouts of an escaped political prisoner, when asked), lying would produce more happiness (or cause less pain) than telling the truth. See also Kant, consequentialist (of system of morals) and utilitarianism.

Desire. That which people wish for or long for. According to Mill, people long for pleasure and happiness.

Dignity. That quality in a person which commands or deserves respect. According to Mill, a sense of dignity is one factor that would prevent those who have experienced, and enjoyed, intellectual pleasures from exchanging them for purely physical ones.

Glossary

Direct perception (of the rightness or wrongness of an action). The idea that human beings can perceive that an action/proposed action is right or wrong without the need to judge it by moral principles.

Directive rule (of human conduct). Rule that directs or guides human actions. According to Mill, this is utility or happiness.

Dunce. Person of limited intellectual ability, limited understanding. An educated person would not exchange his life, and his preferred pleasures, for those of a dunce.

Duty. That which the law, or a set of moral principles, requires/obliges us to do.

Education. This has an important role to play in ensuring that people are as concerned about other people's happiness as they are about their own.

End. That which is desired or aimed at. Happiness and absence of pain are what people desire, and so are the ends of human action.

Ends in themselves. Things or beings, such as human beings, who/that are, or are regarded as being, worthwhile in themselves and not means to an end.

Epicurus/Epicurean. Epicurus (341–270 BC), a Greek philosopher, whom Mill invokes as an advocate of utilitarianism. While this is true of Epicurus himself, Epicureanism is associated with indulgence in purely physical pleasures.

Ethical standard. Moral principle by which an action can be judged right or wrong.

Ethics. A set of moral principles that tell us what our duties are.

Expedient. That which is considered useful or convenient for accomplishing a specific purpose, such as promoting happiness. It is often distinguished from/contrasted with what is just, but Mill takes a different view in his discussion of justice in Chapter V of *Utilitarianism*.

Experience. See observation and experience.

Faculties. Powers, abilities.

First principle (of morality). The basic principle of a moral system: for example, the principle of utility.

First principles (of the sciences). The basic principles of particular sciences.

Fool. A person lacking sense or judgement. An educated person would not exchange his life, and his preferred pleasures, for those of a fool.

Fundamental principle (of morality). Used interchangeably with first principle of morality.

General good. The good of society as a whole. See also general happiness.

General happiness. Utilitarianism is not concerned only with promoting the agent's own happiness (hedonism), but with promoting general happiness, that is the greatest happiness of the greatest number of people. Mill stipulates that, in contemplating an action, the agent must be impartial between his own and other people's happiness; hence the significance of Jesus' golden rule.

Generically distinct (of justice). Belonging to a different group or class. Mill is referring to the idea that justice is generically distinct from utilitarian principles, a view which he challenges in Chapter V of *Utilitarianism*.

God. Mill is thinking of the Christian concept of God, and argues that, if God's purpose in creating the world was his creatures' (human beings') happiness, then there is no incompatibility between utilitarian morality and Christian belief.

Godless. Not based on religious principles. Mill deals with the accusation that utilitarianism is a godless moral system, because it does not base the supreme law of morality on the revealed will of God. He argues that there is no incompatibility between utilitarianism and the revealed morality of a perfectly good God, and that the purpose of Christian revelation is to enable people to discover what is right for themselves.

Golden rule. Mill considers that Jesus' teachings, 'So whatever you wish that men would do to you, do so to them' (Matt. 7.12) and, 'You shall love your neighbour as yourself' (Matt 19.19), express utilitarian morality perfectly. Mill's utilitarianism emphasizes concern for the happiness of others, which is to be treated as at least as important as one's own. See also general happiness and general good.

Greatest happiness principle. The principle that right actions are those which maximize the happiness of the greatest number of people. However, for Mill, who distinguishes between higher and lower pleasures, this is not just a matter of the largest quantity of pleasure.

Happiness. Utilitarianism is concerned with promoting happiness, which can mean different things to different people. For Mill, it does not come from a (sustained) state of pleasure, but is to be found in a well-balanced life, in which a variety of sources of pleasure, such as intellectual pursuits, the affection of family and friends, and engagement with the concerns of society are available, and from which pain, restrictions on liberty and threats to security and property are absent. Mill maintains that (as the nineteenth century went on), such a way of life was available to growing numbers of people, although imperfect laws and institutions denied it to others. There is also the point that following utilitarian principles, and trying to promote the happiness of others, brings happiness to the individual.

Hedonism. Selfish concern with promoting individual pleasure.

Higher faculties. Intellectual abilities. It also includes the idea of using these faculties to pursue intellectual pleasures, such as history, art and poetry.

Higher (of pleasures). More worthwhile pleasures, which are those associated with the intellect, and which educated people prefer.

Impartial. Fair, not favouring one more than another. Utilitarianism requires people to treat other people's happiness as being as important as their own.

Imperfect obligation. An obligation, such as the duty to practise generosity, which is not owed to any particular person.

Implanted (of feeling of duty). The idea that a feeling of duty, and moral feelings generally, are developed through education, rather than being inborn. This is Mill's view.

Inferior (of pleasures). Less worthwhile pleasures, purely physical pleasures.

Inherent. That which is a natural or integral part of.

Innate (of feeling of duty). The idea that a feeling of duty, and moral feelings generally, are inborn, rather than being developed through education.

Intuitive (of moral principles). The idea that, if moral principles are innate, people will naturally perceive the moral principles they should adopt and (without the need for moral reasoning) whether a proposed action is right or wrong.

Jesus. Founder of Christianity. Mill considers that some of his teachings are wholly in keeping with utilitarian principles. See also golden rule.

Justice/just. Treating people fairly, people being treated fairly or receiving their due. Mill discusses the issue of whether justice ultimately depends on utility in Chapter V of *Utilitarianism*, and concludes that it does.

Kant, Immanuel (1724–1804). German moral philosopher,

who propounded a moral system in which, unlike utilitarianism, actions are right in themselves, irrespective of, not because of, their consequences. See also consequentialist (of system of morals) and deontological (of system of morals).

Law. In *Utilitarianism*, in addition to its usual meaning, it refers to a moral law or principle.

Legal rights. People's entitlement under the laws of their society, such as receiving protection for life and property.

Legislation. The enacting of laws, laws that have been enacted.

Lower grade (of existence). A life spent in pursuit of non-intellectual pleasures. Mill maintains that educated people, who enjoy intellectual pursuits, would not exchange their way of life for one that involved pursuit of purely physical pleasures, even though satisfaction might come more easily and they would be less conscious of the world's imperfections.

Lower (of pleasures). Less worthwhile, non-intellectual pleasures.

Means. That which leads to, gives access to, a certain end. Mill argues that virtue, for example, which many people regard as an end, is in fact a means to the end of happiness.

Mill, James (1773–1836). Father of John Stuart Mill and utilitarian philosopher, who worked for the East India Company and wrote a history of British India.

Moore, G. E. (1873–1958). Moral philosopher, professor of philosophy at the University of Cambridge and author of *Principia Ethica*.

Moral belief. Moral principle.

Moral duties. What we are required to do by the particular moral system to which we subscribe. See also duty.

Moral instinct. A natural tendency or inclination to regard certain things as right or wrong, and to do them, as opposed to a rational faculty which uses reasoning to decide whether something is right or wrong.

Moral judgements. Judgements made on the basis of moral principles.

Moral obligation. What we are required to do by the particular moral system to which we subscribe.

Moral philosophy. Branch of philosophy concerned with moral issues and the general principles of morality. It can be concerned with trying to decide what is right or wrong and why we should adopt/follow a certain set of moral principles, or, more narrowly, with the nature of moral argument (what people are doing when they say that a particular action is right or wrong) and the meaning and use of such moral terms as 'right' and 'good'.

Moral principle. See principle (moral).

Moral standard. Moral principle.

Moralist. One who enquires into, teaches, or practises morality.

Morality/morals. System of moral principles, (principles concerning) what is right and what is wrong.

Mystical. In *Utilitarianism*, it is used to refer to the belief that the conscience works mysteriously.

Natural faculty (of moral judgement). A natural ability to determine what is right and wrong. See also moral instinct.

Naturalistic fallacy. The moral philosopher, G. E. Moore, accused Mill of committing this fallacy in Chapter IV of *Utilitarianism*: 'if he confuses "good" which is not ... a natural object, with any natural object whatever, then there is a reason for calling that a naturalistic fallacy; its being made with regard to "good" marks it as something quite specific, and this specific mistake deserves a name because it is so common' (G. E. Moore, *Principia Ethica*).

Nearer good. More attainable, but less worthwhile, good; choosing to pursue purely physical pleasures instead of more valuable, intellectual ones.

Noble (of feelings). Admirable, fine, decent.

Noxious. Harmful.

Obligation. See moral obligation.

Observation and experience. This relates to the idea that moral principles are, or should be, based on our experience of life and our observation of human beings and their needs. See also *a priori*.

Old and New Testaments. Mill refers to both in the context of Christianity only.

Order of precedence. Moral principles may conflict. Utilitarianism can use its first principle, the principle of utility, to resolve such conflicts. Moral systems, which lack a first principle, will need an order of precedence, showing the relative importance of their moral principles.

Pain. Suffering or distress. Utilitarianism holds that right actions are those which promote pleasure and/or prevent pain. See also happiness.

Perfect obligation. An obligation, such as the duty to keep a promise, in virtue of which a corresponding right to require our fulfilling it resides in some person or persons.

Perfectly good (of God). The idea that (according to Christian belief, with which Mill is concerned) God is absolutely or all-good.

Pleasure. That which gives enjoyment or satisfaction. Utilitarianism holds that right actions are those which promote pleasure and/or prevent pain, and which, therefore, bring happiness. At the level of preventing pain, this may involve (apart from dealing with issues of purely physical pain) removing such factors as restrictions on personal liberty and social inequalities, which make it hard for some people to experience pleasure. Sources of pleasure differ from individual to individual, and, for some, a succession of purely physical pleasures would bring happiness. However, promoting such pleasures did not interest Mill, who believed in different qualities of pleasure. Those associated with the intellect are more worthwhile, and happiness is to be found in a life that includes pleasures of this kind.

Precept. Maxim or rule prescribing/guiding conduct.

Principle (moral). Important rule prescribing/guiding conduct.

Principle of utility. The first principle of utilitarianism: that actions are right to the extent that they promote pleasure and (the greatest) happiness, and wrong to the extent that they promote pain.

Private affections. Family relationships, friendship.

Public good. The well-being of society, the wider community.

Public opinion. General opinion in society, which can help to ensure that a moral system is accepted and followed.

Quality (of pleasure). The worth or value of pleasures. Mill distinguishes between higher and lower pleasures, and the quality of pleasure is more important than its quantity.

Quantity (of pleasure). The amount of pleasure, as opposed to its quality.

Rational faculty. Human reason, human beings' ability to reason.

Religion. Mill is concerned with Christianity and the Christian concept of God.

Revealed will of God/revelation. What (people believe) God has chosen to disclose to human beings. In *Utilitarianism*, this is discussed in relation to morality. See also godless.

Rule utilitarianism. Utilitarianism in which the principle of utility functions as an ultimate standard, against which to test secondary principles/rules, and to decide between them when they conflict. Mill did not believe in the necessity of 'reinventing the wheel' of morality every time an action is contemplated; some secondary principles have been shown to promote general happiness, and should be followed. The advantage of rule utilitarianism is that it uses past experience, enables moral decisions to be made quickly, and does not require calculation of the possible consequences of individual actions. The disadvantage is that this indirect approach does not focus on the happiness potential of individual actions, so that it may lead to actions which do not produce the greatest possible happiness.

Sanctions (external and internal). In *Utilitarianism*, a moral system's source of authority and that which enforces it. According to Mill, the main sanctions available to utilitarianism are those available to other moral systems: public opinion and individual conscience. Thus, utilitarians need to persuade society to accept utilitarianism, so that its principles will have the support of public opinion and will become embedded in people's consciences.

Secondary principle(s) (of morality). Moral principles or rules which are based on, or derived from, a first moral principle. Obvious examples are those forbidding murder and theft. Mill makes the point that past experience shows that following such rules promotes general happiness. Therefore, we do not need to go on testing them against the principle of utility in every new situation where they apply. We only need to invoke the principle of utility where these secondary or principles conflict with each other. See also rule utilitarianism.

Sensual indulgences. Pursuit of purely physical pleasures.

Social arrangements/institutions. The laws, governmental institutions and social practices of particular societies. Mill makes the point that, where these are unsatisfactory, they will impede promotion of general happiness.

Socrates (c. 470–399 BC). Greek philosopher, who features in the works of Plato, and who devoted his life to the pursuit of philosophical truth. In relation to the issue of higher and lower pleasures, Mill argues that Socrates' choice of pleasures is to be preferred to that of a fool, just as a human being's is to a pig's.

Subjective. Individual, relating to one particular person.

Subordinate principle(s) (of morality). See secondary principle(s) (of morality).

Summum bonum. The chief or highest good, to which human actions should be directed. For utilitarians, this is general happiness.

Superior (of pleasures). See higher (of pleasures).

Supreme law (of morality). The highest law or principle of morality. See also God, godless and revealed will of God/ revelation.

Standard of morality. See criterion of right and wrong.

Test of right and wrong. See criterion of right and wrong.

Transcendental. Being beyond, existing apart from, the material world; relating to, belonging to, God.

Transcendental moralists. Moralists who believe that morality needs to be based on religious beliefs/principles. See also God, godless, revealed will of God/revelation.

Ultimate end. For utilitarians, this is happiness/general happiness.

Unjust. See justice/just.

Utilitarianism. A consequentialist moral system, which holds that acts are not right (or wrong) in themselves, but only to the extent that they promote pleasure/happiness and prevent pain. Utilitarians differ as to whether the principle of utility should be applied directly to decisions about individual actions, or used as a basic principle against which to measure other principles/rules, and to decide conflicts between them. See also act and rule utilitarianism.

Utilitarian formula. Utilitarian morality.

Valuable (of pleasures). See higher (of pleasures).

Vicissitudes. Changes of fortune, ups and downs of life.

Virtue. Goodness, moral excellence, which some regard as an alternative end to happiness. However, Mill argues that, although pleasure/happiness is the only thing that people desire as an end, utilitarians value virtue highly as a means to that end. If they accept utilitarian morality, those who are virtuous, and who attach importance to doing the right thing, will be diligent in promoting it.